Noteworthy Pubs, Taverns & Saloons of Colorado

D0117244

KAREN O'NEILL EARLEY

Published By

COLORADO ADVENTURE PUBLICATIONS

Noteworthy Pubs, Taverns & Saloons of Colorado

Library of Congress Catalog Card Number 95-69882

ISBN 0-9647300-5-7

Copyright© 1995 Karen O'Neill Earley

Publisher: Colorado Adventure Publications
             P.O. Box 360
             Florissant, CO 80816

Editor: Tanna Shontz

Cover Portrait Photo: Rocky Mountain Photo Works

Photos: Karen O'Neill Earley
         Bill Forbes
         Jorie Earley and Wiebke Wesseler

Cover Design, Art & Production:
         Ben & Barbara Teel
         Teel & Co. Electronic Publishing

Printer: Johnson Printing
           Loveland, Colorado

Printed in the United States of America

First Edition

July 1995

Health and long life to you
Land without rent to you
A child every year to you
and if you can't go to heaven
at least may you die in Ireland.

Sue Powell
Illustrator

Acknowledgments

This book would not have been possible without the help and support of my family; my editor Tanna Shontz, a kindred spirit, (who by the way, moves mountains); my trusted benevolent printer and consultant Craig Nelsen; my graphic artist extraordinaire Ben Teel and his wife and associate Barbara; my professional photographer Bill Forbes; my long-time friend, artist Sue Powell; and my computer wizard Mike Belding.

Dedication

To Kevin and Jorie,
my husband and daughter,
who shared the vision,
provided the support, and
avidly hunted saloons with me.

To my Mom and Dad,
Jerry and Ellie O'Neill,
who instilled in me
a desire to seek adventure
and an appreciation of good books.

Noteworthy Pubs, Taverns & Saloons of Colorado

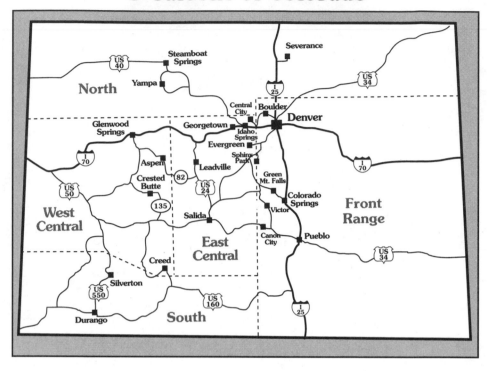

Contents

Introduction

H ISTORICALLY, pubs, taverns and saloons have played a significant role in the shaping of America. From the early colonial taverns, coffee houses and grog shoppes to the saloons of the old West, these establishments not only housed the lost virtues of yesteryear, but also supported the growth and development of the community.

For this guide, I have chosen to seek out Colorado's best, to provide you with the latest information about the most unique and cherished pubs, taverns and saloons throughout the state. Additionally, I have included a few brew pubs of "the new West." The enterprises represented here have been selected on behalf of their uniqueness or grandeur, historical value or authenticity, atmosphere, off-the-wall quality, or possibly even their reputations, past and present.

This is a thirsty undertaking, I know. However, rather than serving as a good excuse for a perpetual toast, I am bringing you this compilation of places to "wet your whistle," while touring the beautiful state of Colorado, to enable you to add a unique feature to your travel. Moreover, the timing is right. Modern society is promoting moderation when it comes to drinking alcoholic beverages. Thus, an appreciation of these establishments for the mere value of their history, setting, menus, entertainment and ambiance, is appropriate, in addition to quenching your thirst!

An historical perspective

The original colonial taverns were actually called "ordinaries." These establishments served a variety of purposes and were as necessary to the establishment of a new town as the blacksmith, general mercantile, pharmacy, and yes, even the church. In fact, for a new town to be legally established in colonial times, it was required that someone erect an ordinary which had to be placed as close to the meeting house (church) as possible—a far cry from the building ordinances of today. The ordinaries were important to society because they provided a place for travelers to seek refreshment and rest, very much needed between stagecoach stops. They were also a locale for the townspeople to convene, communicate, trade, join in camaraderie and warm up after church.

One of the first and most popular alcoholic beverages to be served in America was rum, commonly called "Kill-devil." Rum punch was frequently ladled in taverns. "Flip" was also a favorite drink–made with beer, sugar, molasses or dried pumpkin and flavored with a dash of rum. This concoction was stirred with a red-hot loggerhead which heated the drink and caused it to foam. Cider was also consumed in great quantities, along with ale.

Here in Colorado, the earliest libations consisted of rum, bootleg whiskey and locally brewed beer. Saloons were the most prevalent drinking establishments, springing up like wildflowers wherever gold or silver was discovered. Near the mines, makeshift saloons were erected, followed by gambling halls, and then the town. To give some sense of this phenomena, consider Leadville in 1879, when the town was just two years old– "It was a boisterous mecca for 20,000 miners, replete with 82 saloons and 35 houses of prostitution; yet already the first signs of stability had appeared there–a public school and seven churches."[1] In addition to liquor, many of the saloons provided meals, lodging, gambling and dance hall girls... Back in colonial times, the local ordinary or tavern also doubled as the first post office. Mail carriers would drop the town's mail on a table and let the villagers rummage through it for their own. (Unclaimed mail became interesting pastime reading for locals.)

Today, pubs, taverns and saloons are still abundant with opportunities for meeting new people, learning about the community, taking refreshment and enjoying entertainment. The act of partying, tippling, partaking, toasting, celebrating, carousing, imbibing, nipping and the like continues to be one of America's favorite pastimes. Fortunately, we are now aware of the health and social benefits of temperance.

---

[1] Wilson, D. Ray, (1990). *Colorado Historical Tour Guide*

How to use this guide

For your traveling convenience, the book is divided into sections, representing geographical areas of Colorado. The featured pubs, taverns and saloons are listed by section under the heading of the town in which they are located. Information provided includes the overall rating and type of establishment, general directions, address and phone, hours of operation, meals or not, which credit cards are accepted, and if children are welcome. Following this information will be a general description to convey the entry's individual appeal and notoriety. Of course, suggestions for future editions are welcome.

Each establishment has been rated on the quality of its service, ambiance, decor, uniqueness and authenticity, based on a scale of 1-5, designated by *'s, with 1 * indicating it is worthy of inclusion and 5 *s indicating that it is worth going out of your way for! In instances where significant beer sampling was required, I was able to garner the assistance of certain "beer connoisseurs" to avoid finding myself under the table (or dancing on top of it...). Please let the proprietors know that their places were recommended to you; they'll appreciate your patronage even more.

Happy touring and bottoms up!

About the Author

Karen O'Neill Earley has lived in Colorado for the past 13 years and is originally from Southern California. She now lives with her husband and daughter in Florissant, Colorado. While serving for eight years as coordinator for Faculty and Staff Development at the University of Colorado at Colorado Springs, Karen created a program for faculty and staff called "The Colorado Exchange." This is when she developed an affinity for traveling and exploring Colorado. Since her tenure at the University, she has semi-retired to the Rocky Mountains, does some development consulting, and continues to seek adventures in Colorado.

The Golden Bee
Colorado Springs

*****Pub, Directions: South from Colo. Springs on I-25, take the 115 Hwy to the Broadmoor exit, go west, it becomes Lake Avenue, follow toward the Broadmoor, turn right at 1st Street, 1 Lake Ave., 719-577-5776, Hours- 11:30 a.m. to 1:30 a.m. everyday, all credit cards accepted, Kids OK with adults.*

THE Golden Bee is unparalleled, the finest pub in Colorado. More than an authentic English pub, the Bee is an experience. Its decor is opulent, its reputation worldwide, its libations superlative, its cuisine delectable, and its atmosphere teeming with tradition.

The Bee actually began as a pub in England and was then literally transported to New York City in the early 1800's to set up business in the London Terrace section. The bar ended up being dismantled and put in storage when the business had to make way for an apartment complex. Fortunately, the company assigned to decorate the Broadmoor Hotel in the late 1950's ran across the treasure in an old warehouse. Today, the Golden Bee as we know it rivals the best pubs in England and is a part of the Broadmoor Hotel.

In keeping with pub settings, the Bee is nestled, somewhat cavernously, beneath the Broadmoor International Center. Old spirits barrels and a grog tub welcome you as you venture in. In the Bee you'll discover the most magnificent African mahogany bar, gantry and ornate carvings from the 19th century. Once-upon-a-time gas-like chandeliers illuminate the elaborate ceiling, and original English prints adorn the walls. You'll also find horns, steins, tankards and other assorted vestiges of the mother country. (You may feel as though you've just crossed the Atlantic.)

Photo by Bill Forbes

3

The Golden Bee

Photo by Bill Forbes

According to manager Steve Dimond, the Bee is most noted for the traditions it has established and people-many from around the world-have come to expect. The waitresses, believe it or not, throw bees. Patrons do not have to catch them, they just stick and hang on for the ride (they're actually appliqué souvenirs). Patrons also love the sumptuous Golden Bee cheese spread and crackers that are served at each table. But what truly draws the crowds, every night, are the sing-a-longs.

Famed piano players like Jim Rowe and Bud Kreuzer perform each night from 8:30 p.m. to 1:15 a.m., playing favorite tunes and ballads while the audience joins in. Songbooks are provided, and no one seems shy or out of tune after a yard of beer. That's right, one yard. The Bee boasts an original "ale yard" from the Daphwood House of

Jim Rowe, piano man

Photo by Bill Forbes

The Golden Bee

Buckinghamshire, and replicas are served to the patrons. A yard of imported beer or ale, 48 oz., goes for $12.75 and $10.25 for domestic. A half-yard, 24 oz., goes for $9.75 or $8.25, respectively. For those who aren't quite as thirsty, you might go with a pint, $5.00, or a stein, $4.00. On draught are Whitbread Ale, Guinness Stout, Bass Ale, Watney's Red Barrel, Newcastle Brown Ale, and Coors Light. Bottled ales include Beck's, Molson, Heineken, Amstel, Warsteiner, and Clausthaler. In addition to ales, the full service bar provides the finest malt Scotch whiskies, specialty drinks and wines. O'Doul's also available.

Pub food is served with a variety of soups & salads, sandwiches and pub specials like Steak & Potato Pie, Braised Corned Beef and Cabbage, Beef & Kidney Pie, Shepherd's Pie, Tureen of Chili and the Ploughman's Lunch. Prices range from $3.00 to $11.75. Be sure to leave room for a dessert or two, like an English Trifle or Hot Apple Pie with Wensleydale Cheese.

Phantom Canyon Brewing Co.
Colorado Springs

*****Brew pub, Directions: Corner of Pikes Peak and Cascade in downtown Colo. Springs, 2 E. Pikes Peak, 719-635-2800, Hours-11:00 a.m. to 12:00 a.m. M–Th., Fri. & Sat. 11:00 a.m. to 2:00 a.m., Sun. 9:00 a.m. to 10:00 p.m., Meals, MC/Visa/AE/Disc., Kids OK with adults.*

EUREKA! The Phantom Canyon Brewing Co., which opened in December of 1993, is a novel brew pub of the "new West." Moreover, it is a stellar addition to this collection of "Noteworthy Pubs, Taverns & Saloons of Colorado." Perhaps it is because the Phantom depicts a little bit of each–a little bit pub, a little bit tavern and a little bit saloon...

This eclectic combination is evidenced by the English pub-style food and ambiance, the tavern ales along with the huge copper vats, and the rustic saloon hardwood floors and exquisite back bar.

The place is teeming with character. Be prepared to have the varied aromas awaken your senses to a new experience!

All of this takes place under the roof of an historical, downtown 1901 brick building, which was originally home to the Chicago Rock Island and Pacific Railroad Offices. Subsequently, it was known as the

Photo by Bill Forbes

Cheyenne Hotel. The metamorphosis to a "premier brewing and restaurant company" was no small feat. Proprietors Tony and Anna Leahy will attest to that. In fact, they were able to save the building from being demolished by just one day.

Phantom Canyon Brewing Co.

Owners Tony and Anna Leahy

Launching drinking establishments in Colorado Springs has long been an uphill battle, as the town was legally temperate from the 1870's on. However, alcohol was commonly prescribed for medicinal purposes which explains the multitude of pharmacies in early Colorado Springs.[1] Even today, ordinances ban drinking on the streets of Colorado Springs.

Tony and Anna hail from Milwaukee where Tony was most recently a chef, and Anna was in restaurant management. Tony's inherent Irish appreciation for fine ales, along with both of their gregarious styles, the talents of brewmaster Erik Jefferts, the

Photo by Bill Forbes

expertise of manager Joel Collins, and a committed staff, have turned the Phantom into a true Colorado Springs adventure.

---

[1] Sprague, Marshall, (1961). *Newport in the Rockies*

Photo by Bill Forbes

Phantom, which is the namesake for that notorious character who "did away with" occasional travelers on the highway to Cañon City, offers a well-rounded assortment of its own ales featuring Queen's Blonde Ale (named after Queen Palmer), Hefeweizen, Cascade Amber Ale, The Phantom I.P.A. (India Pale Ale) and Zebulon's Peated Porter. Non-drinkers take note: they also brew their own root beer. The bar, which is one of those beautiful old Brunswicks, has an unusual bar top. It's made of Wyoming limestone imbedded with fossils.

The menu features a lavish assortment of appetizers, soups, salads, pastas, pizza, and delectable luncheon entrees, some of which include; Beer Braised Pot Roast of Beef, Chicken Pot Pie baked with fresh

Phantom Canyon Brewing Co.

Photo by Bill Forbes

Photo by Bill Forbes

Photo by Bill Forbes

tarragon, Fish and Chips battered with Queen's Blond Ale, Shepherd's Pie of Braised Lamb and Root Vegetables, Pan-fried Knack and Brat served with sauerkraut. Lunches range from $2.95 to $8.95. Dinner entrees include items like Shrimp sautéed in a Chilean Roasted Corn Sambal, Pan-Fried Trout, Char-Broiled Atlantic Salmon glazed with honey and pecans, Mesquite Smoked Prime Rib-to name a few-and prices range from $6.95 to $16.95. Last but not least, the award winning desserts: "Black and Tan" Cheesecake Brownie served with ice cream, chocolate sauce, and cinnamon creme anglaise, along with other assortments of cheesecakes, beer bread pudding, tarts, flans and sorbets–Yum!

Tours of the brewing facilities are available on Saturdays from 1:00 p.m. to 3:00 p.m.

Gus' Tavern
Pueblo

****Tavern, Directions: I-25 to the Abriendo exit, north 1/2 block to Northern, cross it & go 1 block to Mesa, right to corner of Mesa & Elm, 719-542-0756, Hours- 10:00 a.m. to 2:00 a.m. everyday, Meals, No credit cards, Kids OK with adults.

MORE than a neighborhood bar, Gus' Tavern is a legacy laden with history. From the Italian heritage and "family" values, to the schooners, shots and Dutch lunches, this place is characteristic of how taverns once were. Luckily for us, Gus' still is.

Indeed, it is probably the most distinctive tavern in this book. The building was built around 1895, served as a church, and was later utilized as a CF&I Steel Mill Office. It has been Gus' since 1925, beginning as a delicatessen/grocery store during prohibition. Once the lid was off, Gus' made the Guinness Book of World Records for having sold more beer than any other tavern in the United States (based on its square footage). This may be because three shifts of workers from the CF&I Steel Mill patronized the tavern.

Today Gus' serves much of the original clientele–those that are still living–plus a huge following of their descendants. It is loved by the locals, who comprise a good deal of the population of Pueblo, in addition to the former Italian neighborhood of the Bessemer area. And, it has become a favorite for those of us who have come to experience Gus' and to relish those famous Dutch lunches.

A Dutch lunch is a platter of ham, salami, and provolone cheese, stacks of soft French bread, chili peppers and relishes. They run $5.50 for a small, (serves

2) and $7.00 for a large, (serves 3-4). Schooners of beer, which used to be called "two-fers"–went for two quarters and your second shot was free. Today schooners go for $1.75; not bad for 18 ounces of beer!

Gus' Tavern

Picture of Gus presides over bar

Gus' is owned and operated today by Alfredo "Freddy" Agostine Masciotra, Gus' son. Freddy has worked and lived at the bar since 1943. He was born in the house next door, began helping out with chores there when he was eight, and started tending bar when he was seventeen. Freddy's older brother Harvey also worked at the bar from 1937 until 1963–the year he died. Sadly too, Gus passed away in 1965. Freddy has carried on the tradition at Gus', being careful to preserve the ambiance of the tavern over the years. This is apparent, as the place exudes a powerful feeling of a bygone age.

The tavern is handsomely furnished. The walls are lined with historical photos which help recapture the past. If one is lucky, the past may also happen to be sitting at the bar. That's where I found Phil Vigil, also known as "The Mayor." As a child, Phil used to

shine shoes at Gus'. Now he's a businessman with KG Men's Store. I also ran across Rocco Anthony Carleo, who is actually called "Mose" and his younger brother Leonard "Bugger" Carlo. (sic)

L to R- Mose Carleo, Colleen Carlo Verhey, and Bugger Carlo

Mose and Bugger's roots go way back at Gus', when they used to work for CF&I along with their mother Rose–she was the first female crane operator. Although fifty or so years have passed, Mose, with Leonard's help, is still able to remember what it was like. Some of it can be printed and well... Today, Mose is retired from the steel mill, (he also helped out at Gus' part-time), and Leonard is an entrepreneur who has owned several taverns himself over the past thirty years. It's not surprising that his place, called "Leonard's Bar" in Colorado Springs, is renowned as a popular "neighborhood" bar.

Freddy says everyone is welcome at Gus'. It's known as a "family kind of place." They've always catered to people from all walks of life, and that's part of what makes Gus' so special.

Gray's Coors Tavern
Pueblo

***Tavern, Directions: I-25 to the 6th St. Exit, follow 6th west to Elizabeth, go left to 4th St., it's on the corner of 4th & Eliz. 515 W. 4th St., 719-544-0455, Hours-9:00 a.m. to 2:00 a.m. Mon.-Sat., 10:00 a.m. to 8:00 p.m. Sun., Meals, No credit cards, Kids OK with adults.

COORS Tavern, known as "Home of the Original Slopper," is an old time tavern located on the edge of downtown Pueblo. The building was built in the late 1800's and was originally a carriage house. It was converted into a bar by the Shafers in the early 1900's.

The tavern was heavily patronized by the railroaders–the rails ran right through what is today the Tavern's parking lot–and during prohibition it served as a sort of speakeasy with the upstairs as a bordello. (The upstairs has since been removed.) After prohibition it resumed as a thriving tavern, and it was then that the Coors Brewery and Mr. Dolf Otterstein, who ran a Coors distributorship in

Pueblo, purchased the Tavern. It was dubbed the Coors Tavern and sold Coors beer exclusively. Subsequently in 1935, John and Joe Greco leased the Tavern from Coors, and it became known as a "hoppin' place."

For years it was also known as the longest bar in Colorado. (Today the kitchen takes up some of that space; however, the bar is still long!) The Tavern witnessed a great deal of Pueblo's history and was visited by many senators, congressmen, and notable figures. John Greco maintains that the busiest day the Tavern ever saw, in the forty-

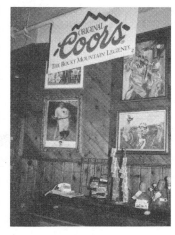

Gray's Coors Tavern

seven years that he owned it, was when President Kennedy made an official visit to Pueblo. The motorcade came right by the Tavern, the street was lined with spectators, and it sold more than 1000 burgers that day.

The Grecos passed on a legacy in the Coors Tavern when they sold it to Don and Gary Gray in 1983. The Grays have continued to preserve the unique character of the place, and Don has added a fine sports collection which complements the theme of Coors Field.

Today the Tavern still serves Coors, along with Bud and Michelob, on tap. Other bottled beers are available, and as I mentioned, they are noted for having the sloppiest hamburgers around. A Slopper is a hamburger on an open-face bun, doused in green or red chili, and smothered with cheese and onions. (I'm told people travel far and wide for this delicacy.) Additional menu items include regular burgers, burritos and sandwiches. Prices range from $1.50 to $4.95. Chili may be purchased to go, red or green, by the pint or quart from $3.50 to $7.00.

Kate's
Cañon City

**Saloon, Directions: North of Hwy. 50, corner of 4th and Main, 331 Main, 719-275-1141, Hours-4:00 p.m. to 2:00 a.m. Sat.-Thu., Fri.-Noon to 2:00 a.m., No meals, No credit cards, Kids OK with adults til 9:00 p.m.

KATE'S is located in Cañon City, a quiet little town famous for its beloved Apple Blossom Festival, among other things. Located off Highway 50 between Pueblo and Salida, Kate's is a convenient sojourn for those going rafting, skiing or simply visiting the tourist attractions of the Arkansas Valley, Pueblo, Cañon City or the Royal Gorge.

Apparently this was the role the building played in the past, having been one of the finer hotels in Cañon. Built around 1874, the saloon section actually served as a bank for the first few years, while the upstairs was the hotel, and the basement was originally a storefront. The bank then moved across the street, and the hotel lobby was located on the first floor. Today, the whole main level is "Kate's," and it offers a host of diversions. There are five pool tables, foosball, pinball, darts and two bars.

In addition to the saloon, which is furnished with some unique olive cane-style chairs and olive carpeting, there are four other sections: the band area, two pool rooms, a dart area, and a bar in the back. Needless to say, there's room! The place is filled with clever decorations such as antique signs, off-the-wall clothing, and old sports equipment. Above the bar is a remarkable old tapestry straight out of "The Canterbury Tales."

Kate Kelly has been proprietor since 1991 and also serves as a city council member. Her assistant manager is Roy Voss who also doubles as bartender. In

addition to domestic brews, Kate's features Elk Mountain Ale, George Killian's, Pete's Wicked Ale, and Honey Brown, to name a few. Live music is provided each Friday and Saturday night and usually features country, jazz, rock or blues. Two of the favorite featured acts are Wes (a band originally from New Orleans) and Papa J and the Boomers. Wednesday and Thursday are Karaoke nights.

Zeke's Place
Victor

VICTOR, founded in 1893, is famous for its gold mining history and for being the boyhood home of Lowell Thomas, news commentator, author and world traveler. In the heart of this historical mecca is where you'll find Zeke's Place. Zeke's has been around since the early days, literally, having relocated four times throughout the century. Today, it resides in what once used to be the Stope Cafe and it (and Victor for that matter) remains unscathed by the gambling phenomenon that has occurred in nearby Cripple Creek.

Les Mattson, proprietor, purchased Zeke's in 1990. He brought a great deal of experience with him, gained by running several establishments in Alaska, California, Utah, and Nevada over the past forty years. Many of Zeke's patrons will remember Ohrt and George Yeager (Ohrt's father), who owned the bar for much of the time following Zeke Bennett, its namesake. Les fondly acknowledges that, "Ohrt and George left a great legacy."

The place has that typical bar atmosphere, yet with its 11 cafe tables, it also lends itself to family clientele. The dark paneling and log siding give Zeke's an authentic aura; there are mounted wild animals,

historical mining photos and bar memorabilia about. Oh yes, Hamburger Bill lives here, too. Zeke's, long famous for its delicious hamburgers, has always had a following (and still does today). Many patrons can still envision Ohrt lining up the pickles, lettuce and tomatoes–quite methodically. Well, apparently Hamburger Bill existed on Ohrt's hamburgers, and when he passed away, his ashes were placed in a bottle and mounted above the bar at Zeke's.

Les is a chef, and now Zeke's offers a broader menu, including breakfast, lunch and dinner. There are specials everyday (occasionally prime rib on

The Rendezvous

Zeke's Place

Saturday for $9.95), and there are summertime bar-
becues on the patio out back. I can attest that the
breakfasts are hearty and tasty (breakfast prices
range from $3.00 to $7.95), and the Spinach Ravioli,
a dinnertime special, is sumptuous. Zeke's is a full
service bar; tap beers include Bud, Red Wolf, and
Millers. They also serve O'Doul's.

Recreation opportunities include a pool table, darts and games. Music consists of a jukebox with country and mixed music, and occasional live bands.

Wayne Rankin,
Victor resident

The town of Victor sports several major events. Donkey Derby Days, in conjunction with Cripple Creek, is held in June. Victor Gold Rush Days, run in mid-July, and the Hill Climb (stock cars) is held the last weekend in July. For more information about these events, contact the Victor Chamber of Commerce at 719-689-3553.

Pine Gables
Green Mt. Falls

THE Pine Gables Tavern appears a bit enchanted, nestled as it is in the forests of Green Mountain Falls. In this pristine setting, just west of Green Mountain Falls lake, the Tavern is located in a building which dates back to 1889.

Originally, the wooden structure housed the Oklahoma Lodge, and served as a boardinghouse with a drug store and boat rental downstairs. Community activities centered around the place, and the soda fountain was the meeting spot for kids. According to historian Jan Pettit, Green Mountain Falls was a dry town. It wasn't until the 1960's that ordinances

**Tavern/Kitchen, Directions: West 15 miles from Colorado Springs on Hwy. 24, 10530 Ute Pass Ave., 719-684-2555, Hours-Noon to 2:00 a.m. everyday, Meals, No credit cards, Kids OK with adults.

were changed and part of the building, which became known as the El Pueblo Building, was then converted to the Silver Tongue Devil Saloon. Today, we know it as the Pine Gables Tavern.

Green Mountain Falls has long been a summer retreat for tourists as well as a transportation stop. It is located part-way up Ute Pass, the old travel route for Ute Indians, stagecoaches and the Colorado Midland Railway. The Midland depot used to be situated right next to the lake. Today a marble marker designates this spot.

Green Mountain Falls and the Pine Gables remain a favorite stopping off place for locals and tourists. New owner Linda Mardosz has kept the historical look of the Tavern and spruced up the dining area. In addition to the tavern and dining room, there is a pool room and dance hall area. Pine Gables is noted for bringing in superb country and rock entertainment, and the tradition continues every Wednesday, Friday, and Saturday night (some Sundays, too). There's usually no cover charge, and the bands begin about 9:00 p.m. Frequently featured are High Trail Riders, and Axis, two of the area's favorites.

Available brews consist of Red Wolf, Bud, Bud Light, Miller, and Coors Light on tap and a wide array of both foreign and domestic bottled beers. Pine Gables is a full service bar, noted for their Bloody Marys. They are also known for their Tavern Specialty- chicken wings, served with celery & carrot sticks, sided with ranch dressing (mild, medium or hot). Other menu items include sandwiches, burgers and pizza. Prices range from $2.00 to $12.95.

Wynkoop Brewing Company
Denver

*****Brew pub, Directions: I-25 to the Auraria Exit, becomes Market St., left on 18th St., 1634 18th St., 303-297-2700, Hours-Mon.-Sat. 11:00 a.m. to 2:00 a.m., Sun. 10:00 a.m. to 12:00 a.m., Meals, MC/Visa/AE/Diners, Kids OK with adults.*

WYNKOOP is the grandfather of them all, Colorado's first brew pub, thanks to a couple of intrepid visionaries–John Hickenlooper and Jerry Williams. One-time geologist and geophysicist respectively turned "brewpubeers", they provide Colorado with a new genre of beer drinking. Not only is it dapper to drink off-the-wall beers, enjoying the flavor, aroma and texture of an ale brewed right on the premises, but it's great fun!

The Wynkoop is the namesake of Edward "Ned" Wynkoop, a founder, the first sheriff of Denver, and a U.S. Army Officer who served as liaison and friend to the Indians. The Wynkoop is located in a lower downtown (LoDo) historical building built back in 1899. (It's just across the

street from the Union Station.) The massive brick building was originally the J. S. Brown Mercantile, which provided Denver with supplies including "stoves, fabric, canned goods and various household items."

Since 1988 it has been the number one brew pub in Colorado, featuring a pub restaurant, two curvaceous bars, brewing vats & other paraphernalia. The pub also boasts the finest billiards hall in Colorado–which also serves as an art gallery–banquet rooms, and a comedy sports club, to boot.

Jorie at Comedy . . .

Wynkoop Brewing Company

The decor is original, with pressed tin ceilings, oak paneling and maple floors. Dining, drinking and brewing take place on the first floor. Fun and games, browsing and drinking take place on the second floor–in the prodigious billiards hall which hosts the original Victorian back bar from the old Tivoli Brewery. Laughs are in the basement where you'll find the Comedy Sports of Denver.

"Fresh Beer, Fine Food, Fair Prices," is the Wynkoop's motto. Indeed, seven to nine varieties of beer are on tap and brewed with "the choicest hops,

malted barley, yeast and water," before your very eyes. Their flagship beers consist of German style beers, Wilderness Wheat and Railyard Ale. English tap ales include India Pale Ale and the St. Charles E.S.B. (Extra Special Bitter). The darker beers are Sagebrush Stout, the

Splatz Porter and the Scottish Ale. Additionally, they make their own alfalfa mead (honeymooners take note!), hard cider, barley wine and a non-alcoholic root beer.

The menu is large and varied with pub cuisine and Wynkoop specialties, all made from scratch. The menu includes appetizers, soups and salads, stews, pot pies, burgers, sandwiches, sausages and pasta. Featured fare includes the likes of Creation from the Black Legume, Shepherd's Pie, Fish & Chips, Pojoaque Valley Green Chili Stew, Beef Stout Pie, Bangers & Mash, Pasta Ewaldo, The Chicken Koop, the Brewer's Burger and the Buffalo Burger. The house specialties boast Brew Plate Specials, The Creature Feature, Something Catchy, The Hunter's Chicken, Smoked Pork Tenderloin, The Tail End of a Legend and The Porter's House Steak. Prices are reasonable, ranging from $1.50 to $16.95, with generous portions–all true to their motto.

Certainly fun is to be had at the Wynkoop. Moreover, they have established an off-the-wall tradition. They celebrate the birthday of the Wynkoop each October with a unique event called the "Running of the Pigs." You'll have to see it to believe it!

Buckhorn Exchange
Denver

*****Saloon/Restaurant, Directions: I-25 to Colfax, east to Osage, right on Osage to 10th, 1000 Osage, 303-534-9505, Hours-Mon.-Fri. 11:00 a.m. to 10:00 p.m., Sat. 5:00 p.m. to 11:00 p.m., Sun. 4:00 p.m. to 9:00 p.m., Lunch served 11:30 a.m. to 2:00 p.m. weekdays only, dinners 5:30 p.m. to 9:30 p.m. Mon.-Th, 5:00 p.m. to 10:00 p.m. Fri. & Sat., 4:00 p.m. to 9:00 p.m. Sun., Credit Cards accepted, Kids OK with adults.*

THE Buckhorn Exchange is the oldest steakhouse and saloon in Colorado. Known for its "dry-aged beef steaks, marvelous buffalo prime rib, tantalizing baby back ribs and various other buffalo, elk and game specialties," it also happens to be a superb saloon and an historical museum. (It is a designated historic landmark on the National Register of Historic Places.)

Established in 1893, it is a truly amazing place and apparently so was its founder, Henry "Shorty

Scout" Zietz. Shorty "was a cowboy, a big-game hunter, and a member of Buffalo Bill's famed band of scouts. He worked in Leadville for Horace and Baby Doe Tabor, was given the name Shorty Scout by the famous Indian Chief Sitting Bull, was a friend and hunting companion of President Teddy Roosevelt and is generally regarded as one of the most colorful figures of the early West."

At the age of thirteen Shorty joined Buffalo Bill Cody's Wild West Show. After remaining with the show for ten years, he worked for Horace Tabor in the Matchless Mine in Leadville. He then settled in Denver, and in 1893 obtained the first liquor license in Colorado and started the phenomenon known as the Buckhorn Exchange. It actually had several names over the years, beginning as the Rio Grande Exchange. It also served as a grocery store and lodge during prohibition and the depression, (there was a secret passageway for patrons to use if the police showed up). It has thrived as a saloon and steakhouse ever since.

In 1938, Henry received a ceremonial visit from Sitting Bull's nephew, Chief Red Cloud at the

Buckhorn Exchange

Buckhorn Exchange. Along with 30 mounted members of the Sioux tribe in full battle regalia, Chief Red Cloud presented Shorty with Sitting Bull's Colt .45 revolver and the sword taken from the body of General George Armstrong Custer by Chief Sitting Bull at the fatal battle of Little Big Horn.

The sword and revolver are no longer in the restaurant; the Zietz family took them when they sold the place in 1978, but you will find over 500 taxidermy items (animals and birds) on display, of which 235 are large animal heads or whole animals. Also on display are 125 antique firearms, some truly one of a kind, and rare Native American artifacts. One room, called the "Buffalo Room" has been devoted entirely to mementos of Buffalo Bill.

In the midst of it all, you can dine. Many of the dining tables are the original poker tables of days gone by. The bar, which was originally downstairs, has been moved to the second floor, which now serves as the saloon and parlor. It's a spacious room, filled with Victorian furnishings and historical artifacts. The bar, made in 1857 of hand-carved white oak, was brought to the United States from Essen, Germany, by Theodore Zietz, Henry's father.

The saloon serves an array of the finest beers–with Moosehead on tap–cocktails and premium wines. Non-alcoholic beverages such as Sarsaparilla, Ginger Beer, Cutter, etc. are available. They also provide some special coffee drinks–Jameson Irish Cream Coffee, Spanish Coffee, Mattie's Silk along with finishers like espresso, cappuccino, Night Capp

Buckhorn Exchange

and Orange Zest, to name a few. In the evenings, you can hear the sounds of Roz Brown, an accomplished autoharpist, in the parlor. He performs folk songs, old West ballads, and sing-a-longs.

And last but not least, the Buckhorn Exchange is one of the finest restaurants around. The raved-about food varies from wild game to the choicest steaks to succulent baby back pork ribs. Exotic appetizers such as fried alligator tail, marinated rattlesnake, and buffalo sausage are

great starters, not to mention those famous Rocky Mountain Oysters. Dinner prices range from $18.00 to $39.00. Lunches include items like "Grandma Fanny's renowned pot roast sandwich, a rave-gathering honey mustard chicken sandwich, five enormous burgers, bratwurst or rib platters, main course salads and, of course, the Buckhorn's world-famous bean soup." Lunch prices range from $6.50 to $8.95. To top it all off, they serve a wide array of delectable desserts.

The Hungry Toad
Boulder

Photo by Bill Forbes

***Pub, Directions: From Denver take Hwy. 36 to Boulder, left on Arapahoe, right on Broadway, 2543 N. Broadway, 303-442-5012, Hours-11:00 a.m. to 11:00 p.m., Mon.-Fr., Sat. & Sun. 10:00 a.m. for brunch, Meals, MC/Visa /AE/Diner's/CB, Kids OK with adults.*

THE Hungry Toad is a traditional English pub. Here you'll discover fine ales, authentic English cuisine, distinctive architecture, and that "pub camaraderie", which is characteristic of its ancestors over in England. True pubs, not unlike our Colorado saloons, give one the impression of stepping back in time.

The Hungry Toad was established in 1991 by Terry Morton, a native of England. He modeled it after its sister pub in London, also dubbed "The Hungry Toad." Terry has done well in re-creating for us what the English have enjoyed for centuries. The pub is located in a 1910 building which originally served as a grocery store, pharmacy and a restaurant. The old brick building is tucked away among the trees and shrubs and lends itself to enchantment. Inside you'll find a cozy dining room bedecked with signs from England. The barroom is slightly raised

Photo by Bill Forbes

and is handsomely furnished with hardwood floors and a mahogany bar, bar stools, bar tables, and captain's tables.

Photo by Bill Forbes

The Hungry Toad

Happy hours are a delight at the Hungry Toad. Typical of English pubs, this place serves as the neighborhood bar, too, and affability abounds. The staff, headed by general manager Bruce Garber, goes out of its way to see that everyone is having a good time, and that's especially true during happy

Photo by Bill Forbes

hour. English pints go for $2.50 from 4:00 p.m. to 6:00 p.m. Monday through Friday. Libations include Odell's 90 Shilling, Fullers E.S.B., Toad's Premium, Double Diamond, Newcastle Brown, and Guinness Stout, a European draft beer of the month - Black and Tan on my visit - plus an assortment of imported and domestic ales and a full service bar.

The Hungry Toad is also distinguished for its cuisine. From starters, salads, sandwiches and burgers to entrees, burritos, and pasta, there's something for everybody, even the kids - there's a "Tadpole" menu. The Toad specialties are Fish and Chips, London Broil, Cornish Chicken & Mushroom Pie, Shepherd's Pie, Vegetarian Pot Pie and Steak Diane. Prices range from $2.95 to $15.95. They also feature a brunch on Saturday and Sunday from 10:00 a.m. to 3:00 p.m. with prices ranging from $6.25 to $7.75.

Bruce's Bar
Severance

Founder Bruce Ruth and the author

***Bar/Restaurant, Directions: Hwy. 14 East to Severance, 970-686-2320, Hours-10:00 a.m. to 11:00 p.m. Sun.-Thu., and til 2:00 a.m. Fri & Sat., Meals, MC/Visa, Kids OK with adults.

BRUCE'S. Surely you've heard of it? Home of the "Rocky Mountain Oysters." No, not those slippery things that Mom and Dad eat on the half shell. These oysters are different. They're not grown in the ocean; they're imported from Costa Rica. In fact, Rocky Mountain Oysters are the "finest bulls' nuts in the world," or so I'm told.

Bruce Ruth has owned the tavern since 1957. It was a beer joint/recreation center at that time with one pool table. Bruce transformed it into a restaurant and bar, adding on to it over the years. Today Bruce's is considered something of a phenomenon. It is known for its good food and down-home atmosphere; however, it is infamous for those purported aphrodisiacs-the Rocky Mountain Oysters. People come from all over the world to experience Bruce's and the Oysters, which he has turned into a Colorado tradition.

In addition to the Bull Fries, patrons can enjoy hamburgers, sandwiches and fish & chips, with prices ranging from $1.50 to $6.25. Additional dinner items include; steaks, lobster, shrimp, crab, and scallops. Dinner prices range from $2.00 to $19.75. Don't worry about making reservations for dinner-there's plenty of seating-rows of it.

Bruce's Bar

This is a spot where you can rub elbows with your neighbor, and perhaps even ask him to dance. It seems Bruce's has become quite a honky-tonk on the weekends. The house band called "The Ruthless" plays country music every Friday, Saturday, and Sunday night–with no cover charge. For those who

like to get up and move around, there are three pool tables, various games and two separate bars. Be sure to say "Hi" to Bruce or one of his long-time staff–Betty has worked here for thirty years, and Linda and Dennis have both been here almost twenty-four years!

The Tugboat Grill & Pub
Steamboat Springs

****Saloon/Restaurant, Directions: Hwy. 40 east from Craig or north from Kremmling, becomes the main st.-Lincoln, follow it to Mt. Werner Road, north towards the ski area, 1860 Ski Time Square Dr., 970-879-7070, Hours-7 a.m. to 2:00 a.m. Mon.-Sat., Sun. 9:00 a.m. to 2:00 a.m. (closes in Spring), Meals, MC/Visa/AE, Kids OK with adults.

TUGBOATS in the Old West? Why not?! At least there's water . . . steaming hot springs. Also in keeping with the town's name, you'll find the Harbor Hotel and Steamboat Yacht Club, too. But if the truth be known, Tugboat was a cat. While a conglomeration of bartenders were constructing the saloon in 1972, Tugboat was given "mice duty", which the cat enjoyed, until it was finally overwhelmed and found cornered by the mice one day.

The Tugboat Grill and Pub is a fun saloon/ restaurant with raved-about food, a unique ambiance and "the best nightly entertainment in the valley." The interior is that of a turn-of-the-century Old West saloon, with an authentic bar (bullet hole and all) originally from the Log Cabin Saloon in Baggs, Wyoming. Even more interesting is the off-the-wall decor featuring a wide array of trophies, from huge, not-so-seldom seen wild animals (including many new species-the work of "frustrated taxidermists"), to the abundant celebrity and sports photos–patrons of the Tugboat all–as well as a hat collection that keeps getting better (and bigger).

The Tugboat Grill & Pub

Proprietors
Hank Edwards
and Larry Lamb

Hank Edwards and Larry Lamb are proprietors, good friends and great hosts. They, along with Jack, the bartender extraordinaire, and the friendly staff, make everyone feel at home. Tugboat serves "the best breakfast in town" from 7:30 a.m. to 11:30 a.m., and it includes their famous Omelettes, Egg on a Muffin, Pancakes, and specialties like the Tugboat Favorite, Huevos Rancheros, Eggs Sonora,

Hangover Helper, and Steak and Eggs, prices ranging from $2.95 to $7.95. Lunch and dinner items are served until 10:00 p.m. and include a wide array of appetizers, burgers, Mexican dishes, soups & salads, sandwiches, and fish favorites. Prices range from $1.95 to $6.50.

Evening entertainment varies from rhythm & blues, country, rock & roll to blues and reggae–seven nights a week during ski season.

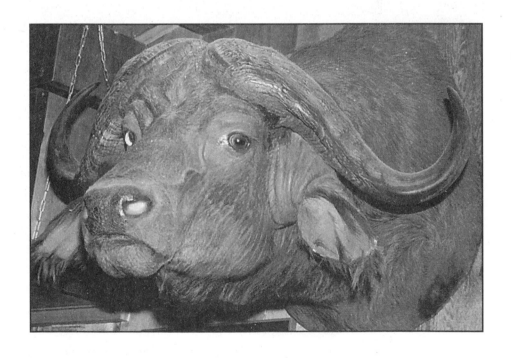

Old Town Pub
Steamboat Springs

****Saloon/Restaurant, Directions: Hwy. 40 east from Craig or north from Kremmling, becomes Lincoln, 600 Lincoln Ave., 970-879-2101, Hours-Sun. 9 a.m. to 1:30 a.m., Mon.-Sat. 11:00 a.m. to 1:30 a.m., Meals, MC/Visa/Disc/AE, Kids OK with adults.

THE Old Town Pub is located in what used to be the Albany Hotel, dating back to 1904. Since its hotel days, the building has also been home to Steamboat's first hospital, the local post office, a movie theater, a dry goods store, an electrical store, a dance hall, and even the Odd Fellows Club. In 1969 it was converted into a restaurant known as the Cameo, and finally in 1984, two creative entrepreneurs transformed the establishment into the "Old Town Pub."

These entrepreneurs are the notably energetic and gregarious Paul "Loui" Antonucci and Joe Pete LoRusso–former Boston construction workers who put their skills to work in converting the place into the charming restaurant and pub that it is today. In addition to hard work and ingenuity, their success is

One of the owners, Loui Antonucci

due to their business savvy, some of which Loui gained while earning a degree in business. Today, when they're not managing the bar full-time, Loui is mountain biking, exploring canyons, or climbing fourteeners, and Joe is usually falling down–from the sky that is. Joe–an Airborne veteran–is a sky diver. When he's not diving, he's teaching it or bailing people out of jail (he owns Valley Skydivers and serves as Steamboat's bail bondsman).

Old Town Pub

Photo by Jorie Earley

The pub, where meals are also served, is finely furnished in rich dark wood with two bars—one of which originated in Oak Creek, Colorado. The decor features captain's tables and chairs, bar tables and stools, original hardwood floors, a dart board area, and interesting signage. The restaurant is spacious yet quaint, with plenty of windows which afford a view of downtown activity in Steamboat. The pub and restaurant are partially separated by dividing walls which can be removed to create one large room. This is done when popular local bands and acts from out of town (Michael Martin Murphy, Mick Fleetwood & Stevie Nicks to note a few) are the featured entertainment.

Breakfast, lunch and dinner are served. Prices range from $3.95 to $6.95 for breakfast and lunch, with dinners going for $5.95 to $19.95. Breakfasts include items such as Pub Eggs, Omelettes, the Kitchen Sink and Huevos Grande. Lunches feature a special variety of soups & salads, burgers and sandwiches. Dinners (the Pub is noted for being an especially good steak house) include an assortment of burgers, seafood, prime rib and steaks, Tex-Mex, pasta and baby back pork ribs-the slow cooked, fall-off-the-bone kind.

And last but not least, the libations...Old Town Pub is considered a "headquarters for Margaritas" where patrons can choose from Blue Agave Blends, 100% Agave Premium, and 100% Agave Super Premium–Sauza Tres Generaciones–the rarest and finest tequila in the world. Beer connoisseurs, too, will be pleased with the selection of draft beers-Bud, Bud Light, Breckenridge Avalanche, Pyramid Amber Wheat, Tabernash Denargo Lager, along with bottled Corona, Heineken, Anchor Steam, Samuel Adams, Amstel, O'Doul's & Thomasbrau, to name a few.

Antlers Bar
Yampa

Yampa, Hwy. 131 on the way to Steamboat Springs

The Antlers Bar is a "must see" for saloon hunters. It is quite historical, picturesque and more than a little bit different. I guess what makes it different is its peculiar owner, Mike Benedict. He's

quite a character and has owned the bar "forever." If you're into old time saloons, drop by on your way to Steamboat Springs (Hwy. 131), and take a peek. You won't be disappointed, but be prepared for anything!

The Buck Snort Saloon
Sphinx Park

Photo by Bill Forbes

*****Saloon, Directions: from Denver–Hwy. 285 south, past Conifer to Schaffer's Crossing, turn left & go 6.5 mi. From Woodland Park–Hwy. 67 north, left at Deckers on 126 to Pine, turn right on 4th St. (the center of Pine), then right on Elk Creek Road & go 1.5 mi., 15921 S. Elk Creek Road, 303-838-0284, Hours are seasonal–generally 12:00 p.m. to 12:00 a.m. in summer–call ahead otherwise, Meals, No credit cards, Kids-absolutely.*

For those who have yet to discover it, the "Buck Snort Saloon" awaits you! Tucked away in Sphinx Park, just east of the old railroad town of Pine, this saloon is a delight and a historical treasure. Once you leave the highway at Pine, you begin to think you might have missed the turn-off—-keep going. Your clue will be the cabins precariously hanging from the cliffs, like the boulders, one of which is the namesake for Sphinx.

Photo by Bill Forbes

Once known as the Sphinx Park Mercantile, providing supplies for the residents of this one-time resort community, this rustic log structure now houses the Buck Snort Saloon, one of

Photo by Bill Forbes

Colorado's most renowned mountain bars. It is famous for its delicious food, mountain brew, great hospitality, and fun-loving customers. The canyon in which it's nestled is a world-class rock climbing mecca with the famous Elephant Rock just down the road. (The Rock Climber's Guide is kept at the bar for reference.)

Mountain Jack and Lynnette Hargiss are the new proprietors of the Buck Snort. Jack is somewhat of a native, born in Denver yet raised in Pine. He actually attended Pine's two-room schoolhouse and

The Buck Snort Saloon

remembers coming to square dances at the Buck Snort when it was still the mercantile. Recently, Mountain Jack purchased the Buck Snort from Tom

Paton, who had been the owner for thirteen years. Tom had re-established the place, (it has been the Buck Snort for the past twenty-five years) and transformed it into the popular saloon that it is today.

You'll find the staff to be very friendly. Indeed, this is one of the Buck Snort's many attributes and has certainly played a part in their propensity for winning awards: Best

Photo by Bill Forbes

Mountain Bar in 1985, 1989, 1990, 1991–this award given by Westword (Denver News and Arts Weekly) was finally discontinued because the Buck Snort

Photo by Bill Forbes

kept winning it! The Buck Snort was then placed in

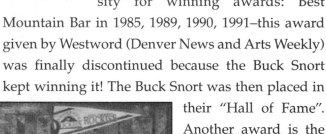

their "Hall of Fame". Another award is the Denver Post Critic's Pick: Best Place to Take an Out-of-Town Guest in 1987, not to mention their numerous printed and broadcast rave reviews. (I guess it's no surprise that I'm here!)

The entry to the Buck Snort leads directly into a bright and airy game room which was

Photo by Bill Forbes

the original mercantile building built in the early 1900's, followed by the saloon/restaurant.   Log-on-end barstools provide unique seating, along with the many cable-reel tables. The patio out back allows patrons to enjoy the soothing sounds of Elk Creek. Graffiti covers the rough-sawn walls along with historical and climbing photos, celebrity pictures, and huge wild animals.

A juke box plays a full range of music, and on Saturday nights live music is provided–usually a mix of country/rock and comic musicians. For many years, patrons were drawn here to listen to the band "Sashay", composer of "The Buck Snort Song."

The menu has something for everybody, and the prices are right. The fare includes health food as well as mouthwatering Buck Burgers (beef), which are a favorite. Most meals range from $2.75 to $7.95, featuring the likes of the Climber's Special, the Burritos, Philly Cheese Steak (You'll think it's from Philly!), the Forest Fire, Mountain BBQ and the Buck Snort T-Bone Steak ($16.95), to name a few. There are

many famous and imported brews available – Watney's, Coors, Coors Light, Molson– and they also feature their own Antler Ale, brewed just for them by the Wynkoop Brewery.

Photo by Bill Forbes

Little Bear Tavern
Evergreen

*****Saloon/Nightclub, Directions: I-70 west of Denver, Main Street, Evergreen, 303-674-9991, Hours-11:00 a.m. to 2:00 a.m. Mon.-Sat, til midnight Sun., Meals, MC/Visa, Kids OK with adults til 6:00 p.m. on Sat/Sun.*

MORE than a great mountain bar, the Little Bear Tavern is an entertainment extravaganza. It is nationally known as "THE" place to go in the Rocky Mountains for great music and a good time–this popular establishment has been awarded "Rowdiest Mountain Bar," as well as "Best Mountain Bar," by Westword. Indeed, live music is provided almost every night of the year, with three concerts on Saturdays and two on Sundays. The music runs the gamut from country and rock 'n roll to rhythm &

blues, funk, and heavy metal. The tavern features local bands and pioneered the concept of bringing in national acts–Count Basie was one of them, way back when. Little Bear also used to be a place to go for Dixieland music. Today

you'll be more likely to hear the sounds of Dave Mason, Leon Russell, B.J. Thomas, Jim Messina, The Platters, Willie Nelson, Michael Martin Murphy, The Subdudes, Firefall, Randy Meisner, and David Wilcox...

Little Bear has been owned by Kenny and Judy Jeronimus for the past twenty years and is managed by David Stubbs. The tavern is in an imposing old timber building and is complete with the original hardwood floors, a three-sided bar, abundant captain's tables & chairs, wooden loft seating, and a notorious stage—bedecked with lingerie. The place is also home to a bear (check him out in the buggy upstairs!). There's a license plate collage and other interesting signage dispersed throughout.

Little Bear Tavern

Upstairs, if you venture past the balcony, you'll find a secluded pool room with three tables and video games.

The building was built back in the late 1800's and originally housed a trading post and drug store in

one half and a church in the other. It survived a fire in the 1920's thanks to the local residents' bucket brigade from Bear Creek. Today, it is all Little Bear, a boisterous boozer with

a cafe/grille on one side and the tavern on the other. Food is served from the grille, which is noted for having "the best pizza and burgers in town." (I can attest to the pizza!) Other food fare includes subs, sandwiches, nachos, chili and wild appetizers with prices ranging from $2.75 to $15.75. The bar is full service with many versions of Coors on tap and a variety of bottled imports.

Concert tickets may be purchased by calling Ticketmaster.

The Red Ram
Georgetown

****Saloon/Restaurant,
Directions: Off Highway
70, approx. 40 miles west
of Denver-Exit 228, 606
6th Street in Historic
Georgetown, 303-569-
2300, Hours-Tues. thru
Sun. 11:00 a.m. til 9:00
p.m., Bar open until...,
Meals, MC/Visa/Diners/
Disc/CB/AE, Kids OK
with adults.*

Long known as the place for local skiers to stop to and from the slopes, the Red Ram has a more distinctive history laden with ties to silver mining, banking and, not surprisingly, women of ill-repute.

It all began in 1876 when Charles R. Fish, "Colorado pioneer and mining and properties investor", built the Bank of Clear Creek County in Georgetown. It was originally a wooden structure with Barney Hannigan's Saloon in the rear portion, Eagle's Clothing Store adjoining and rooms for rent up above. In 1887, a fire destroyed much of the building, despite the heroic efforts of the local fire department, and eventually the building was rebuilt in 1889, this time with brick. The 100' x 80' structure was known as Fish Block. It housed the bank and post office, the Pease Grocery Store, and the upstairs was utilized for temporary residence and professional offices. Around 1925 the Pease Grocery was converted to

the Loop Bar, and finally to what we know today as the "Red Ram."

Back in the late '50s, the basement was also used as a sort of German Tavern. It is reported that many wives would deliver their husbands to the upstairs saloon, just to have them slip downstairs to the additional tavern and perhaps, saunter even further. For downstairs, in the rathskeller, is located the "whore door", connecting the tavern via tunnels to purported houses of ill-repute in Georgetown.

Today you'll discover the Red Ram continues to be an authentic, beautiful old time saloon. Their mascot proudly presides near the magnificent back bar, and there are distinguished wooden signs that add to the character of the place. In addition to the saloon part, the Ram loops to the other side of the block where you'll find an additional non-smoking section of the restaurant.

The Red Ram

The Konowe family, proprietors since 1993, continue to make the Red Ram a traditional experience. The brews alone are worth stopping off for. They include the likes of Red Ram microbrews Red Ram Pale and Stout, plus the Silver Plume Beer. Also available are Guinness, Watney's, Pete's Wicked Lager, and Killian's Red.

Everything at the Ram is made from scratch. Patrons can purchase fresh rolls or Red Ram sauces to take home. The luncheon menu features an assortment of appetizers, soups & salads, sandwiches and "Red Ram Burgers", with prices ranging from $2.00 to $7.95. The dinner menu includes the much raved about Chicken Denese, Shrimp Scampi, slow-cooked (mouthwatering) Prime Rib and Lobster Tail to name a few. Dinner prices range from $7.95 to $18.95, and on Wednesday night the Ram features an "all you can eat" Spaghetti Feast for $6.50, $4.50 for Seniors & kids.

With all this great food and drink, you'll be surprised to learn that the "Mother Load," their homemade chocolate ice cream, is what gains national attention. In fact, it's been rated by the New York Times and the New Yorker magazine as one of the top five ice creams in the nation.

Teller House "Face Bar"
Central City

****Saloon, Directions:
Hwy. 119 north from
I-70-just west of Denver-
or south on Hwy. 119
from Nederland, 120
Eureka St., 303-582-3200,
Hours-9:00 a.m. to 2:00
a.m. everyday, Meals,
MC/Visa, AE, Kids OK
with adults.

THIS is the place! There are few who haven't heard of the bar with *"the face on the barroom floor."* The "Face Bar" as it is more widely known, is located in the Central City "Teller House Hotel" which was built in 1872.

From the early days (1859) when John Gregory first discovered gold, to Harry Gunnell's find, and many other strikes, Central City has attracted hordes in search of the precious metal. With the onslaught of gold diggers, it

was evident a hotel was needed. Henry Teller, a lawyer who arrived in Central City in 1861 and established a prominent practice with his brother, commissioned the building. It was pronounced "the

finest hotel between St. Louis and San Francisco."[1] In addition to the hotel, the building originally housed a bank, which was the forerunner of the Rocky Mountain Bank, until the bank was moved to Denver in 1915. A billiards room occupied the place where the Face Bar is today.

Business boomed for the hotel from 1872 till 1900 as the population in the county grew to about 25,000. Following this period and the decline of the silver market, things slowed down for the hotel until 1936 when Anne Evans, daughter of John Evans, second Territorial Governor of Colorado, bought the place and had it restored.

---

[1] Taitt, Mary Sawle, (1990). *Opera House Stories & Teller House Tales*

Teller House "Face Bar"

Legend has it the face on the barroom floor was painted by Herndon Davis of the Denver Post in 1936. He had been hired to help with the remodeling, which included transforming the billiards room into a bar, but fell out of grace with Miss Evans. Banned from the Teller House, and true to his mischievous character, he decided to leave a memento. The face painting is that of his wife, Edna Juanita Davis, and it infuriated Miss Evans. It did not please Mrs. Davis either, because she was then serving as an officer in the Women's Christian Temperance Union. (The impetus for Herndon's artwork stemmed from the 1898 barroom ode, "The Face Upon The Floor" which was performed frequently in days gone by.)

The notorious Muses of Central City who grace the walls of the Face Bar were painted by Pierce Stanley back in 1883. They were discovered underneath wallpaper when Miss Evans was having the hotel

restored. Originally there were eight. Two more were painted during and following the restoration of the murals by Paschal Quackenbush, with the assistance of Poncho Gates.

Today, the saloon remains illustrious, and once again, the hordes come to seek their fortunes-this time with Lady Luck. Central City, along with Black Hawk and Cripple Creek, is one of the few spots where gaming is legal in Colorado. Indeed, you'll find plenty of gambling at the Teller House, but the Face Bar remains the same, and there's a new restaurant, Madeline's, located directly behind the bar in what was once the Lillian Gish Atrium. Meals are served in the Face Bar, too. Breakfast is available anytime, and the menu also features an array of sandwiches, burgers, soups and salads. Prices range from $1.95 to $6.75. On tap are Heineken, Molson Ice, Coors Winterfest, Samuel Adams and Killian's Irish Red. A host of bottled beers are available with prices starting at $1.25 to $2.95 for 22 oz. of beer.

Tours of the historic hotel and adjacent Opera House are available each day from 9:00 a.m. to 4:00 p.m. and are conducted by local historians Mary Sawle Taitt and Dolores Spellman.

The Gold Coin Saloon
Central City

**Saloon, Directions: Hwy. 119 north from I-70 west of Denver or south on Hwy. 119 from Nederland, 120 Main St., 303-277-1900, Hours-8:00 a.m. to 2:00 a.m. everyday, No Meals, No credit cards, No Kids allowed.

IWOULD be remiss if I did not include the Gold Coin Saloon in this book. It is located around the corner from the Teller House Face Bar in the Lady Luck Casino. It happens to be a fancy little saloon, and it is purported to be the oldest in Central City. The beauty of the Gold Coin is that in spite of the surrounding gaming industry, its original character, stemming from 1878, has been well-preserved. Missing however, is Jack Brown–a renowned bartender for over twenty years. Jack passed away about six years ago, and it is clear that he is missed. His legacy continues at the Gold Coin.

The interior of the place is genuine, colorful and classy, from the original hardwood floors, mahogany bar and gantry to the swinging barroom doors and store part up front. The one-man-band player piano is a gem and suits the place along with the pot belly stove, schooner, animal trophies and historical photos.

Apparently one other thing remains the same at the Gold Coin–many of its patrons. The locals boast proudly of this establishment, and it's evident that their camaraderie and unique humor have something to do with the marvel of the Gold Coin. Pick up a copy of "The Little Kingdom Come" while you're

The Gold Coin Saloon

here. There's usually an issue on hand, and it's published "Whenever We Damn Well Feel Like It." This should clue you in to the off-the-wall humor that abounds in this tiny community and perseveres at the Gold Coin.

Available brews include Molson, Molson Ice, Corona, and Heineken, with Miller Genuine Draft, Coors Light and Bud on tap. Draws are fifty cents all the time.

Newspaper photo of bartender Jack Brown

Buffalo Bar & Restaurant
Idaho Springs

*****Bar/Restaurant, Directions: West of Denver on I-70, Exit 214-A, 1617 Miner St., 303-567-2729, Toll Fr. 1-800-477-2227, Hours-11:00 a.m. to 10:00 p.m. Mon.-Sun., Meals, All credit cards, Kids OK with adults.*

THE Buffalo Bar is quite a famous place, tucked away in the old mining town of Idaho Springs. The town was established when gold was first discovered by George Jackson back in 1859. This delightful restaurant/bar originated in 1906 and was known then as John Rohner's Bar and Billiard Hall. (John Rohner is also famed as a former contender for the heavyweight championship of the world.)

As legend has it, John worked next door at the "Worth Bar" and quit when he didn't receive a 5 cent a day raise. He then vowed "to put Mr. Worth out of business"; he bought and remodeled the building next door and turned it into a flourishing business. Today, that building is the main section of the Buffalo Bar. Eventually John Rohner ended up taking over the Worth Bar, adding it on to his establishment. That section is now referred to as the Buffalo Pub.

Buffalo Bar & Restaurant

Kevin peeping

The Buffalo Bar is a cool place. It's replete with original squeaky hardwood floors (the building dates back to 1880), magnificent mahogany bars, back bars and breakfront, beautiful antique stools and hutches, a 1911 player piano, a 1900's peep show,

hunting trophies and memorabilia galore, a 1948 Rockola Juke Box, and perhaps even a ghost. The place echoes with class.

Art and Darlene Rosean, owners for the past thirteen years, say the reason the Buffalo is so popular is because of its food. I can vouch for this. Indeed it is a choice restaurant, in addition to being a great mountain bar. It's a fun place with a friendly staff.

Jorie checking out the cave.

General manager Debra Simmons, along with floor managers Keith and Don, have certainly played a part in the exemplary service offered at the Buffalo.

The lunch and dinner menus are lavish, offering starters, soups and chilies, salad, special sandwiches, burgers, fish, Mexican specials, Buffalo entrees, BBQ favorites, chicken and prime rib au jus. Dinners also feature Italian fare and steaks. For those who haven't ventured to sample Buffalo yet, take the plunge! The meat is described as "USDA Prime #1 Colorado raised buffalo; it is lean and tender, tastes slightly sweeter than beef, and lacks the gamy taste associated with deer and elk. Buffalo is low in cholesterol and fat, and very high in protein." Prices range from $2.50 to $16.95. Tap brews include Silver Plume's Amber Ale and Dunkelweiss Wheat plus a wide variety of domestic bottled beer. Another quality note: well drinks are made with premium liquors.

Silver Dollar Saloon
Leadville

*****Saloon, Junction of Hwys. 24 & 91, located on the main street in Leadville, 315 Harrison Ave., 719-486-9914, 11:30/noon - 2:00 a.m. everyday, No meals, No credit cards, Kids OK with adults.*

STEP into the "Silver Dollar Saloon", and you'll step back in time. This is the original saloon and gambling parlour of Leadville's heyday, virtually unchanged. Not only is the establishment well preserved, but so is the atmosphere. Some of you may sense it when you walk in the door...

Established in 1879, just as silver had become the new pay dirt in Leadville, the Silver Dollar Saloon has been a favorite of miners, gamblers and gunslingers (the likes of Doc Holliday), and even the upper crust of Leadville. It is located directly across the street from the famous Tabor Opera House. Today it is still renowned, a favorite for the locals and an attraction for tourists and writers, some of whom come from all over the world. (Jimmy Buffet pops in occasionally with his buddy, Jack Nicholson.)

Tony Cowfer behind the bar

According to records, the Silver Dollar was originally built by the "Leadville Improvement Company, with H.A.W. Tabor as recorded president." The original name was "The Board of Trade." The first proprietors were Henry Poire and A.B. Miller, until it changed hands in the late 1800's to become the property of John G. Morgan. By 1943, the McMahon family became the proprietors, and today the Silver Dollar Saloon is owned and operated by Patricia McMahon. Pat's son, Tony Cowfer, also lends a hand by frequently bartending and sharing its history with patrons.

Silver Dollar Saloon

The McMahon's have established an Irish tradition at the Silver Dollar, which you'll notice by the artifacts mingled with the historical treasures. St. Patrick's Day is twice yearly celebrated in Leadville. The first is in September with the practice parade and then again on the usually observed March 17.

The originality of the decor in the saloon is stunning. Take note of the superior quality of the magnificent back bar, front bar, two front booths, windbreak and swinging doors. Also of special note are the 3/4 inch diamond dust mirrors made by Brunswick and imported from St. Louis, Missouri, by covered wagon. The back room, now converted

to a dance and pool room, used to be the gambling parlour. In addition, there were gaming rooms upstairs. A dumbwaiter, originally used to serve the patrons in the upper chambers, is located behind the bar. The saloon still possesses two of the original blackjack tables, which are interspersed with social tables, a piano, a stage for live bands, a shuffleboard and a juke box. It's not surprising the Silver Dollar was rated the number one bar in the book "BarHop USA, America Then and Now."

Silver Dollar Saloon

You won't find any silver dollars here, except for a portrait of Rose Mary Echo Silver Dollar Tabor, the notorious daughter of "Baby Doe" and Horace Tabor. She was purported to have burned to death (accidentally by spilt scalding hot water) in a Chicago brothel.

A full service bar offers mixed drinks, wine, and bottled beer, much of which is Irish, along with an assortment of fine Irish Whiskies.

*The infamous con man,
Soapy Smith*

*In memory of
Mac MacDonald*

The Victoria Tavern
Salida

**Tavern, Directions: Hwy. 50 to F Street, go north toward downtown, 143 N. F St., 970-539-4891, Hours- 12:00 noon to 2:00 a.m. everyday, No meals, MC/Visa, Kids OK til 9:00 p.m.

How did this sleepy little town come up with such a winner? Perhaps it is a combination of fate, the railroads, the river, the artists, the locals, a few ghosts, and a creative entrepreneur. Peter Simonson, who hails from Wisconsin, has been tavern keeper since 1981.

The Victoria Tavern is located in the historic district of Salida, next to the Arkansas River. (This used to be the border of Mexico, remember?) Just across the

*Photo by
Wiebke Wesseler*

river was the original train depot– the tracks ran in six directions– and the site of the Monte Cristo Hotel. The tavern still occupies its original building, built around 1903, and it began as the "Victoria Hotel and Tavern."

Today, the tavern is expansive, running throughout the entire downstairs. Upstairs, a few rooms are still available for lodging. The old brick building has retained its historical quality, with some character remodeling added over the years. The ambiance is antique and welcoming. The hardwood floors and peanut shells strewn about give it an unpretentious

The Victoria Tavern

Patron and author at the bar

Photo by Wiebke Wesseler

flavor; however it is grand. Of special note is the impressive molded tin ceiling. The handsome back bar is a JP Paulsen out of Denver, enhanced with some striking newer stained glass works.

The tavern, known far and wide as a very happening place (it's nicknamed "The Vic"), offers much in the way of recreation. There's an original shuffleboard, two pool tables, ping pong in the "way back," as well as big screen TV for sports fans. The Vic hosts Sunday football with Peg, one of the favorite bartenders, and this seems to be a ritual for many of the locals.

A calendar of events is printed to keep patrons informed of daily activities and specials. Boasting of "live music since 1903", the calendar includes a listing of featured bands, some local and some imported, whose music ranges from rock n' roll, country and blues, to jazz and reggae. Live entertainment is featured every Friday and Saturday night from 9:30 p.m. to 1:30 a.m. Here's an interesting note: Fridays are smoke-free at the Vic.

The brew should satisfy everyone's taste, ranging from Bud, Coors, Sharp's and Cheers, to Watney's, Red Hook and Leinenkugels out of Wisconsin. The bar, which is managed by Joan, is full service and happy hour runs from 5:00 p.m. to 7:00 p.m.

Red Onion
Aspen

***Saloon, Directions: Hwy. 82 to Main St., right on Mill St. to Cooper St., 420 E. Cooper St. Mall, 970-925-9043, Hours-11:00 a.m. to 2:00 a.m. everyday (except opens at 11:30 a.m. in winter), Meals, MC/Visa, Kids OK with adults.*

THE Red Onion is the oldest original saloon in Aspen and occupies one of the few buildings that survived the fire of 1941. Since then, the town has literally grown up around the Onion, and the place has helped to establish Aspen's reputation for being a charming and fun place to go. Like several of the grand hotels in Aspen, the Onion is an historical treasure.

The saloon was built during the silver boom in 1892 by Tom Latta. It changed hands several times over the years, and in 1984, David "Wabs" Walbert and Robert "Buddy" Nicholson became the proprietors. Many of its first customers were considered "sporting men, interested in all forms of prize-fighting, wrestling, cycling, and other popular sports of the time." Note the rare collection of tintype boxing photos about the place; many boxers were friends of Tom Latta. In 1947, when skiing became the sport in Aspen, the Red Onion once again became known for being "the" place to go. It evolved

into a night club in the '50s and became a haven for famous musicians, showcasing the likes of Billie Holiday and other blues, jazz and rock'n roll per-

formers. The collage on the rear wall of the restaurant recaptures the night life that transpired over its next twenty years. One patron recounts that when she was partying here in 1961, Jacqueline Kennedy was dancing in the back room.

The interior, in keeping with original saloons, is abundant with dark wood, booths, and a majestic Brunswick bar and gantry. The bar has some unique wooden inlays which were discovered only after one owner "gave it a good cleaning." (Take note of the figures

Red Onion

above the bar that evoke fairy tale images–they're over 100 years old.) The floor is made of tile, and years of patron traffic, and perhaps even a few ghosts, are evident. The ceilings are ornate pressed tin, and the booth table tops are inlaid with patrons' memorabilia; history comes to life with their stories. Indeed a patron recollects "the fishing pole in booth three belonged to the great fisherman, Homer Jaycock, who went blind and could no longer tie flies. The rest of his days were spent in the Red Onion."

Many of these stories have been preserved by Tom Elder, who has managed the Red Onion (R.O.) for the past two years and been an Aspen resident for twenty. Noticing how so many patrons seemed to reminisce when they came in, he initiated an "Alumni Association" of sorts. Anyone who comes into the R.O. and appears to be recounting the past is asked to share his memories in the official "Memoir Book." (Someday this unique piece of literature will be selling in the bookstores!)

The rear portion of the R.O., which was originally used as a gambling room and then a music room, is

now the restaurant section, and the front remains all saloon. The restaurant is famed for its French Onion Soup, Mexican fare and steaks. Also served is a wide array of appetizers, burgers & sandwiches, salads and desserts. Prices range from $1.50 to $10.95. In addition to the daily specials, the Red Onion offers a nightly summer special—a 10 oz. ribeye steak for $10.95. Brews consist of Fat Tire, Red Lady, Bud, Miller Genuine Draft, Bud Light and Leinenkugels on tap and many assorted bottled beers. The bar is full service and cappuccino is available, along with the Red Onion's own special coffee.

Doc Holliday's Saloon
Glenwood Springs

***Saloon/Tavern, Directions: Just south of Jct. I-70 and Hwy. 82 in Glenwood Springs, 724 Grand, 970-945-9050, 10:00 a.m. to 2:00 a.m. everyday, meals 11:00 a.m. to 11:00 p.m., No credit cards, Kids OK with adults.

MEMORABILIA abounds at Doc Holliday's to convey the legend of this infamous dentist/gunslinger and good friend of the Earp's. Because Doc was fond of the drink, it seems most appropriate that a saloon should have been dubbed in his honor. (This is the town where Doc finally succumbed to tuberculosis.) He was also very fond of Big Nose

Kate, and her photo is duly mounted on the wall along with other notorious characters of the time.

Marty Yoder has been proprietor since 1988, and the saloon continues to be popular for its great food and drink, in addition to its namesake. Marty has added immensely to the authenticity and ambiance of the saloon by collecting antiques and historical artifacts

Doc Holliday's Saloon

of the old West. Dark wooden dining tables are situated in the front of Doc's, complemented by the antique 130 year-old-bar and the pool room with two tables and a juke box.

The menu features lunch and dinner. There are appetizers galore and a wide selection of sandwiches and burgers, including "Doc's World Famous Burgers." Prices range from $1.75 to $7.95. In addition, dinners include Mexican fare, steak and seafood. Prices range from $2.25 to $11.95. Drinks include a full service bar, plus brews like Wisconsin's Leinenkugels, Live Kugali's and Lebatts.

DOC HOLLIDAY

Doc's is within walking distance of the famous Glenwood Hot Springs Pools, and it is center stage during the Doc Holliday Day celebration which is held in July. Strawberry Days, which has been a Glenwood Springs tradition since 1897, is celebrated in June.

Old Miner's Inn
Creede

Photo by Bill Forbes

****Saloon, Directions: Hwy. 149 north from South Fork or south from Lake City, middle of Main St., 719-658-2767, Hours–11:00 a.m. to 2:00 a.m. everyday in summer–otherwise call, Meals, MC/Visa, Kids OK.

CREEDE, which lies at the base of Willow Creek Canyon in the northwest San Luis Valley, is famous for its silver mining history and its many legends–the likes of Calamity Jane, Soapy Smith, Bob Ford, Bat Masterson and Poker Alice. As history goes, the town's non-stop raucousness incited Cy Warman to write a poem in 1892.

Creede remains a favorite, quaint, and sometimes boisterous town. There are a few places to wet your whistle, and one you won't want to miss is the OMI–Old Miner's Inn.

As with many of the establishments in Creede, the Old Miner's Inn is located in one of those historical buildings that once was...in this case, it was originally the Miner's and Merchant's Bank built in 1892. The name was later changed to the Old Miner's Bank. Subsequently, the bank was converted to the Creede Post Office until it was relocated in 1976.

From then on, the place boasted the Old Miner's name again, and it happens to be the "coolest bar in town." (You'll find many people will drink to that!)

The OMI is cool, and it's fun. The ambiance is that of an old Western saloon. I thought for sure I'd stumble across Calamity Jane here. Who knows, I may have...

Mike and Susie Mendenhall have recently taken over from Larry Goode. His sister Sandy continues to help manage the place. The owner before Larry was the late Jim Lamb, who was a legend in his own right. Jim was also the leader of the popular band the "OMI Express", and it was while touring with his band that fate took his life in a tragic accident. It was Jim's grandfather, E.B. McCrone, who served as postmaster and had owned the building since 1932.

Classic rock and roll music plays on the juke box and live bands are featured on Friday and Saturday nights (sometimes Weds., too). The OMI Express still

"And There Is No Night In Creede"

Here's a land where all are equal-
  Of high or lowly birth-

A land where men make millions,
  Dug from the dreary earth.

Here meek and mild-eyed burro
  On mineral mountains feed,

It's day all day in the daytime
  And there is no night in Creede.

The cliffs are solid silver,
  with wond'rous wealth untold,

And the beds of running rivers
  are lined with purest gold.

While the world is filled with sorrow,
  And hearts must break and bleed,

It's day all day in the daytime
  And there is no night in Creede.

Old Miner's Inn

performs here, and they continue to be a very popular band, noted for their musical expertise and for having carried on with Jim Lamb's gregarious style.

Mixed drinks (the booze is in the vault), beer, wine and non-alcoholic brews - - O'Doul's, Sharp's and Cutters, can quench your thirst, and the newly-remodeled adjoining OMI restaurant will satisfy your hunger.

Photos by Bill Forbes

Photo by Bill Forbes

Featured fare includes: raved about pizza, pasta, sandwiches, soups and salads. Prices range from $2.25 to $6.25, with a large "Mother Lode" pizza going for $16.95.

Creede is a happening place. For information on year-round sponsored events, contact the Creede-Mineral County Chamber of Commerce at 1-800-327-2102.

Kochevar's Saloon
Crested Butte

***Saloon, Directions: Hwy. 50 to Gunnison, north on Hwy. 135 to Crested Butte, left on Elk Street, 127 Elk, 970-349-6745, Hours 11:30 a.m. to 2:00 a.m. everyday, Meals served 11:30 a.m. to 10:00 p.m. Mon.-Thu. til 12:00 a.m. on weekends, MC/Visa, Kids OK with adults until 8:30 p.m.

ON YOUR way to the "mountain" lies the city of Crested Butte, a quaint, thriving historical community. Usually filled with tourists, students from nearby Western State College, or skiers, you'll find the locals at Kochevar's. I did. That's also where you'll discover the secrets and true essence of Crested Butte–it's been well preserved in this genuine 1896 saloon.

Kochevar's still occupies its original building where it began as a saloon in the front, living quarters in the rear, and a restaurant adjacent. In the late 1890's, proprietor Jake Kochevar planned on also providing a brothel upstairs–in addition to gambling, whiskey and beer. However, his wife put a halt to that notion just as he was beginning to install the bedroom windows. Today, the upstairs remains unfinished. Kochevar's did succeed in providing great enter-

tainment for residents, hunters, homesteaders and the not-so-uncommon gunslingers – some of whom were on the run. Legend has it that Butch Cassidy and his gang were enjoying a game of poker at the front gaming table when they had to make a quick exit. (So hastily that one of the members left his six-shooter lying on the table.) Kochevar's still retains the gun to this day, and it's brought out for special events sponsored by the town.

The saloon is still partially owned by the Kochevar family today. In its authentic splendor, it possesses many of the original gaming and faro tables, and a most interesting clock. Games can still be played at

Kochevar's, including poker. There's a table up front – where Butch sat - along with billiards, shuffleboard, darts and video games.

Available brews consist of Red Lady Ale from the Crested Butte Brewery, Whitbread & Heineken on tap, and other assorted bottled beers. Happy hour runs from 4:30 p.m. to 6:00 p.m. everyday, and meals are available from Karolina's Kitchen which still adjoins.

The Diamond Belle Saloon
Durango

*****Saloon, Directions: Hwy. 160 or 550 to Main St., 1887 Main, 970-247-4431, Hours-11:00 a.m. to 1:00 a.m. everyday, MC/Visa/AE/Diner's/ Dis., Kids OK with adults.*

SALOON enthusiasts will be pleased to discover that Durango is a "gold mine" when it comes to superior drinking establishments. From 1800's saloons to Irish pubs, sports bars and honky-tonks, Durango has it all. There are literally too many quality establishments to include, so in keeping with my authentic saloon hunting genre, I have chosen to feature the "Diamond Belle Saloon." The Diamond

Belle is a classic Victorian turn-of-the-century saloon, which many of you will agree is superior. Apparently Louis L'Amour thought so, he often worked on his novels when staying at the Strater Hotel and enjoyed the libations and respite provided by the Diamond Belle.

The Diamond Belle is located in the Strater Hotel, which was built in 1887. The saloon was named after a notorious prostitute from Silverton. Legend has it that she had a diamond inlaid in her front tooth (she was also known as Diamond Leona). The hotel and saloon have been in the Barker family since 1926. Today, Rod Barker is owner and manager.

The saloon, originally called the Nugget, was first opened in the basement of the hotel, and the pharmacy was located where the saloon is today. In 1957, business savvy on the part of Earl Barker motivated

The Diamond Belle Saloon

him to have the saloon relocated, unbeknownst to his father, who was out of state. The Diamond Belle has been thriving ever since. The saloon is exquisite with a majestic back bar, beveled mirrors, chandeliers, hardwood floors, a piano, and a balcony to offer seclusion or a pleasant vantage point. Portraits of former cocktail waitresses adorn the walls, and the waitresses/bartenders of today appear just as festive.

When the distinguished ragtime/honky-tonk pianists aren't making music—which is every night but Sunday—the stereo is tuned to the country western sounds of K-Frog, often featuring the renowned DJ Kevin O'Neill (where have I heard that name before?..). Sundays you'll be treated to live music, often the local bluegrass sounds of "Heart 'n Soul."

On tap is Anasazi Wheat brewed by the Durango Brewing Company, Coors, Bud, Miller Lite, and Elk Mt. Amber Ale-which is imported from New Jersey and brewed by Anheuser-Busch. Lunch is served Monday through Friday from 11:30 a.m. to 1:30 p.m. only and includes Diamond Belle's Remedy (Chili) and a wide array of specialty sandwiches. Prices range from $3.00 to $6.50. Meals are also available in the hotel restaurant, the Henry Strater.

Rod Barker, owner

Handlebars Saloon
Silverton

*****Saloon, Directions: Hwy. 550 to Silverton, 117 East 13th St., 970-387-5395, Hours, 10:30 a.m. -2:00 a.m.-everyday May 1 through Oct. 31, restaurant til 10:00 p.m., MC/Visa/Dis, Meals, Kids OK with adults.*

TRUE saloon lovers will revel in the "Handlebars Saloon." The epitome of an old Western saloon, from the rustic hardwood floors and bar, mining memorabilia–including the ore car fireplace–Western artifacts and mounted wild animals, to the grizzly bear up on high, you'll savor the wild, wild West. The location is ideal, nestled in the old mining town of Silverton, originally called Baker's Park. Famous for its silver mining history, bordellos and

The Earps

gunslingers, county records show that Doc Holliday was paid $26 to "clean up the town."

The Boden family established Handlebars in 1989. Those patrons sporting a handlebar mustachio will receive a free drink, and the patron's picture will be mounted at the bar.

The building, built back in 1880, originally housed the Posey and Wingate Hardware Store in one section and a bank in the other. Handlebars was converted into a saloon in the late thirties, and at one time it was named Baker's Park Rendezvous, serving as a meeting place for trappers and miners. Today, the front section is home to the Storyteller Indian Store, and in the back you'll find Handlebars.

Handlebars Saloon

Byron Haynie and Kevin O'Neill

It is still one of the favorite rendezvous spots for tourists, locals and occasional celebrities, as Handlebars has a reputation for exceptional food. The menu is varied and some of the featured fare includes: Rocky Mountain Oysters, Huge-O'Onion Rings & buffalo wings-from $4.75-$5.95, salads, soups & chili-$3.75-$5.95, sandwiches & burgers (beef & buffalo)-NY Steak, Old Fashioned BLT, Turkey Avocado Sprouts, and California Dreaming - $5.25-$6.95, baby back ribs & prime rib-$8.25-$8.95. Dinner items also include steaks, ribs, prime rib, honey-dipped/grilled lemon or Cajun chicken, spaghetti, and even halibut-$6.95-$17.95. Leave room for dessert—the famous Handlebar Perfection-made with white chocolate mousse, strawberries, whipped cream & chocolate sauce in a thin wafer! To quench your thirst, there's a full service bar featuring Elk beer, Avalanche, Heineken, and O'Doul's.

Nighttime entertainment includes Karaoke, and on Friday and Saturday nights, patrons can enjoy Country Western music, oftentimes featuring the professional sounds of Byron Haynie from Nashville.

Proprietor Kenneth Boden tending bar

Bibliography

Aird, Alisdair–Editor (1992). The 1992 Good Pub Guide. London: Ebury Press, Random Century House.

Bennis, Benjamin James, (1992). Restaurants from 101 Colorado Small Towns. Colorado: Small Town Publications.

Churchill, E. Richard, (1974). Doc Holliday, Bat Masterson, & Wyatt Earp: Their Colorado Careers. Leadville: Timberline Books, Ltd. CO.

Earle, Alice Morse, (First Pub.1900, reissued 1969). Stage Coach and Tavern Days. New York: Benjamin Bloom, Inc.

Feitz, Leland, (1969). A Quick History of Creede: Colorado Boom Town. Colorado: Little London Press.

Hanson, Neil, (1988). Classic Town Pubs: A Camra Guide. London: Pavilion Books Limited with Michael Joseph Limited.

Rice, Kym S. for Fraunces Tavern Museum (1983). Early American Taverns: For the Entertainment of Friends and Strangers. Regnery Gateway.

Sprague, Marshall, (1961). Newport in the Rockies. Colorado: Sage Books.

Taitt, Mary Sawle, (1990). Opera House Stories & Teller House Tales. Colorado: Minuteman Press.

Wallace, Robert, and Editors of Time Life Books, (1976). The Miners. New York: Time Life Books.

Wilson, D. Ray, (1990). Colorado Historical Tour Guide. Illinois: Crossroads Communications.

To obtain additional copies of this book,
please check with your local bookstore,
or send $15.50,
(includes tax, shipping and handling)
with name and address to:

Colorado Adventure Publications
P.O. Box 360
Florissant, CO 80816